The Grafton Monster

BY GEORGE DUDDING

PUBLISHED BY GSD PUBLICATIONS
Spencer, West Virginia
April 25, 2019

http://www.gdparanormal.com

In Memory of Pamela Jane Dudding
1957-2012

Dedicated to my parents:
John Goethals Dudding
Marcelline Bumgarner Dudding

Graphics Design and Publishing Assistance
by John Dudding

No. 2019-002

© COPYRIGHT 2019, 2022

INTRODUCTION
By the Author

We are finding out that many of these strange, weird monsters seem to be showing up, out of who knows where, in small towns that have nothing more exciting going on. The first eyewitnesses usually seem to experience problems with ridicule and doubt regarding the authenticity of their stories. The monster may make a series of appearances, and then, it vanishes never to be seen again. Could it be that these entities are also showing up in other communities, but the distractions are so great that no one even notices?

Usually, the initial witness or witnesses are younger people that have a known reputation for being credible. In the case of the Grafton Monster, the principal witness was a professional news reporter in his mid-twenties. Witnesses usually try to report their discoveries to the improper—I mean proper—authorities, which are usually the police. Many times this leads to problems, because if the police are skeptics, then everyone else follows along, and the majority of the public will not believe the actual witnesses. Later, when the witnesses take everyone back to the scene of the encounter, it seems that no evidence can be found except mashed down grass or broken tree limbs. The authorities, the local news media, and others occasionally make up their own descriptions of what must have been seen instead of using the description provided to them by the witnesses of what was actually seen.

There are also a bunch of weirdos that always arrive, represent themselves as the real experts, and possess a vendetta against everyone associated with the encounter. These are the skeptics, and they often come to prove, in any way they can, that the incident has something to do with an owl, swamp gas, or a temperature inversion. Occasionally, they might just throw in an arbitrary object, such as twelve-cubic-foot refrigerator sitting along the road, just to throw everyone off, because you can't keep saying everything was a barred owl and maintain credibility.

I had heard of the Grafton Monster, along with other such monsters as the Snallygaster and the Snarly Yow many years ago. They were brought to the forefront in recent years by the *Mountain Monsters* reality TV show. Six years ago, after completing one of my earlier books, *The Tale of the Mason County Mothman*, I began collecting information on the Grafton Monster but could never get to the point of writing a book about the strange entity. Recently, another author pointed out that I had written something on just about everything else and suggested that I do this book, since this monster had reached a certain level of fame after being featured in a video game, *Fallout 76*, that takes place in the background setting of West Virginia. Since I needed a new topic to write on, I decided that the headless monster of Grafton would be a good place to start because I already had a big part of the research completed.

My first move was to create the basic framework of the book to determine if such a book could be written to my satisfaction. The number of pages was not one of my major concerns as long as I could cover the topic without introducing any type of false embellishments or making any attempts to sensationalize the story. Once I had successfully completed that task, I headed to Grafton to dig deeper into the monster's background. That was when things turned rather strange.

On Tuesday, April 16, 2019, my son John and I arrived in Grafton to investigate the legend of the Grafton Monster. I was armed with my Sony digital camera, and John was testing out a Nikon camera that we had just acquired during the previous week. A case containing my paranormal investigation equipment was stashed in the trunk of the Monte Carlo SS in case a need for it arose.

Perhaps, it was partly because I had already done a considerable amount of research before going to Grafton, but I had an uncanny feeling as if I had been there before—a feeling of being in an area of high strangeness. I always have that same feeling when exploring my hometown of Point Pleasant, West Virginia, where the Mothman was first sighted in 1966. From Interstate 79, we took U.S. Route 50 into Grafton and immediately went to Riverside Drive. That was where everything first began fifty-five years ago. We spent quite a bit of time exploring and photographing the two-lane, blacktop roadway, along with the riverbank of the Tygart River, which is the key to understanding the legend of the Grafton Monster. I was trying to imagine what it would have been like to drive along that stretch of road late at night way back then. Afterwards, we moved on to other key points around town to further our investigation.

As we drove through town, we stopped off at several places in the order of which they came, and I soon realized that there was no difference in this investigation and many others in which I have been involved. The townspeople of Grafton simply did not seem willing to talk with strangers about the incident that took place there back in 1964, but it seems that they would whisper about it among themselves.

The local newspaper office was one of our first stop-offs, because its predecessor had once played a role in the initial monster sighting. We spoke with several reporters in an outer office and did not extract any information. Instead, we were directed into a back office where we were introduced to the editor. Even the editor seemed to have no knowledge of the incident with the exception that they had published a story covering the recent theft of a billboard associated with the monster. From that point, we were referred to a downtown coffee shop and the local library.

Our next stop was the local coffee shop, where we ordered drinks and snacks. The coffee shop is known as a hangout for local "Beast of Grafton" aficionados. Our visit there turned out to be positive after the attendants at the counter learned we were investigating the century-old mystery and writing a book. They pointed out that the regulars who often came in to discuss the monster were not present that day, but we should speak to a young woman sitting at a nearby table. She turned out to be a graphic artist with an interest in the cryptids of West Virginia. Her sketchpad was full of visual representations of everything from Mothman to the Flatwoods Monster with everything else in between. She was not able to give us any new details on the case, but she directed me to several vantage points where I could get a good view of the CSX railroad yard and the old Willard Hotel. Afterwards, we headed back out on the street to explore the downtown area, including the Andrews Methodist Episcopal Church, the old B&O railroad station, and the now defunct Willard Hotel.

Once we completed our objectives in the downtown area, we headed across the river to the Taylor County Library, which turned out to be a modern facility. We had learned that the library held microfilmed archives of the *Grafton Sentinel* newspaper that had once covered the story surrounding the appearance of the monster on that fateful night many years ago. A woman greeted us at the circulation desk and offered to help, but like everyone else, she did not seem to have any knowledge of the monster sighting. She did indicate that there had been several others inquiring about the same topic, so she put us in contact with another library worker that had assisted them. This worker had thought far enough ahead to keep copies of the newspaper articles that had been retrieved during an earlier search of their microfilm. It was a welcome turn of events that our mission at the library was fulfilled within fifteen minutes when we were given copies of those news stories.

Upon departing the library, we were able to take out the time to visit two National Cemeteries that were located nearby and to see the grave of the first Union soldier to be killed by a Confederate soldier at the onset of the American Civil War. Then, we made our way three miles south on U.S. Route 119 to the community of Webster and visited the birthplace of Anna Marie Jarvis, who was the founder of Mother's Day in honor of all mothers including her own mother, Ann Reeves Jarvis.

After completion of our mission to learn the truth about the Grafton Monster, we boarded the Monte Carlo SS for the trip back to Spencer, West Virginia, but not before paying the Taylor County Senior Citizen Center a visit where some valuable information was gained.

You will find that I have included, just as I have in my other books, some history associated with both the monster and the community to make it an educational experience. I hope you enjoy reading my latest book, *The Grafton Monster*.

AUTHOR ALONG BANKS OF TYGART RIVER
PHOTO BY JOHN DUDDING

TABLE OF CONTENTS

AREA HISTORY 1
THE GRAFTON SENTINEL 11
THE SIGHTING 12
THE FOLLOWING DAYS 18
EARLY THEORIES 22
NEWSPAPER CLIPPINGS 28
SIMILAR SIGHTINGS 32
GRAY BARKER 40
AN INTERPLANETARY ALIEN 42
AN INTERDIMENSIONAL ALIEN 48
THE MEN IN BLACK 51
FALLOUT 76 53
MOUNTAIN MONSTERS 55
A LOCAL COFFEE SHOP 59
GRAFTON MONSTER BILLBOARD 60
CONCLUSION 64
PRE-RELEASE REVIEWS 66

DEPICTION OF GRAFTON MONSTER INCIDENT

THE GRAFTON MONSTER

"Most of the monsters are based on some sort of mythology. Every culture and even some geographical areas have monsters and mythology that is their own."

–Laurell K. Hamilton, American fantasy and romance writer

AREA HISTORY

Taylor County, located in north-central West Virginia, was formed from parts of Marion, Harrison, and Barbour Counties in 1844 by an act of the Virginia General Assembly. It was named after United States Senator John Taylor (1753–1824) of Virginia. The county seat of Taylor County was Pruntytown from 1844 until 1878 at which time it was moved to the town of Grafton.

Taylor County covers an area of 176 square miles and has a population of 16,859. It is geologically characterized by its V-shaped

GEORGE DUDDING

valleys, narrow flood plains, and steep hillsides. The area was originally populated by a Pre-Columbian group of Native Americans, known as the Adena culture, that lived there during the Woodland Period between 1000 BC and 200 BC. Fur trapper John Simpson was the first recorded white person known to have frequented the area around 1768.

> "...he engaged the services of 19-year-old George Washington to survey the property..."

TAYLOR COUNTY HIGHWAY MARKER

The area presently occupied by the City of Grafton became an early white settlement on the western edge of the Virginia frontier after the arrival of European white man. It was first settled by a Scotch-Irish immigrant by the name of James Current. A local history source states that Current purchased a 1,300-acre tract of land situated at the confluence of Three Fork Creek with the Tygart Valley River on the headwaters of the Monongahela River. After exchanging a horse for the property, he engaged the services of 19-year-old George Washington to survey the property around 1751. James Current was also known to have later become a veteran of the Revolutionary War after fighting in that war around 1778. Current is mentioned in a 1782 census record of the Grafton area even though he lived there much earlier. He is the only Revolutionary War soldier known to be buried at Grafton. His gravesite can be found in the Current Cemetery along Victory Avenue.

"Control of that railroad line was of major importance during the Civil War..."

GEORGE DUDDING

The City of Grafton, present population of 1564, was originally chartered in 1856 and named in honor of John Grafton, a civil engineer who laid out the route of the Baltimore and Ohio Railroad in 1852 across what was then northwestern Virginia. Much of the early history of Grafton is based around its railroad industry. In 1850, the Virginia legislature chartered the Northwestern Virginia Railroad Company to build a railroad line reaching from the Baltimore and Ohio Railroad to Parkersburg, Virginia (now West Virginia) with the stipulation that it pass through the Tygart River Valley. In 1852, Grafton sprung up along that railway and soon became a major railroad town. Control of that railroad line was of major importance during the Civil War because troops and supplies were transferred through the area by rail. As a result, a national cemetery and a military hospital ended up being located there.

At one time, 500 workers were employed by the Baltimore and Ohio Railroad at Grafton, and the town is still a busy railroad town to this day. The architecture of buildings and homes in Grafton speaks of railroad wealth. The six and one-half story Willard Hotel, listed on the National Register of Historic Places, still stands between Main Street and the railroad yard next to the old railroad depot in the downtown area. It was constructed by Grafton attorney and industrialist John T. McGraw in 1911 for the B&O Railroad and named after B&O President Daniel Willard.

THE B&O RAILROAD WILLARD HOTEL
PHOTO BY JOHN DUDDING

The Grafton area was also a prosperous coal mining community many years ago, but the coal mining industry has diminished drastically. Arch Coal recently began operating the Leer Mining Complex nearby, which is a longwall mine that produces coking, or metallurgical, coal used in steelmaking. The mine has been so successful that

GEORGE DUDDING

Arch Coal has just announced plans to open a similar mine in adjoining Barbour County.

Today, the Grafton area is accessible to visitors and tourists by U.S. Route 250, U.S. Route 119, U.S. Route 50, and nearby Interstate 79. An abundance of highway historical markers that commemorate the rich history of the area are found along many of these roads.

CSX RAILROAD YARD IN GRAFTON
PHOTO BY AUTHOR

The Grafton National Cemetery, listed on the National Register of Historic Places, is located at 431 Walnut Street in Grafton. As space became limited there, another cemetery, the West Virginia

THE GRAFTON MONSTER

National Cemetery, was established five miles west of Grafton at 42 Veterans Memorial Lane.

Thornsbury Bailey Brown, the first Union soldier to be killed by a Confederate soldier during the American Civil War, was killed on May 22, 1861 at Grafton, Virginia (later West Virginia). Brown was from the unincorporated community of Fetterman, which was later absorbed into the incorporated City of Grafton. Brown's gravesite can be found in the Grafton National Cemetery.

GRAVE OF THORNSBURY BAILEY BROWN
PHOTO BY JOHN DUDDING

GEORGE DUDDING

Clair Francis Bee (1896–1983), a famous college basketball coach, was born at Grafton. At one point, he also served as a college football coach and was involved in other notable aspects of athletics. After leaving the field of coaching in 1950, he became the author of the popular Chip Hilton series of juvenile sports fiction.

Grafton is the birthplace of Anna M. Jarvis, who was the founder of Mothers Day. On May 12, 1907, Jarvis arranged for a ceremony to be held in honor of her mother at the Andrews Methodist Episcopal Church. The following year, on May 12, 1908, the service was expanded to include mothers everywhere. That church is located at 11 East Main Street in Grafton. It is listed on the National Register of Historic Places and has been designated as the International Mother's Day Shrine. The birthplace of Anna M. Jarvis can be found three miles south of town along U.S. Route 119 at the community of Webster.

"...home to a wide variety of native wildlife and possibly another strange creature..."

THE GRAFTON MONSTER

Taylor County and the City of Grafton are known for their recreational areas including the Tygart Valley River, the 1,740-acre Tygart Lake, Tygart Lake State Park, Valley Falls State Park, and the Pleasant Creek Wildlife Management Area. The Grafton area lies along the Tygart River surrounded by hilly land, dense forests, and small farms. All of these areas are home to a wide variety of native wildlife and possibly another strange creature that is known to stalk the woods around the Tygart River—the "Headless Horror" often called the *Grafton Monster*.

BIRTHPLACE OF ANNA M. JARVIS
PHOTO BY JOHN DUDDING

GEORGE DUDDING

**ANDREWS METHODIST EPISCOPAL CHURCH
INTERNATIONAL MOTHER'S DAY SHRINE**
PHOTO BY JOHN DUDDING

THE GRAFTON SENTINEL

A local newspaper began in the town of Grafton in 1870 and eventually became a daily paper, the *Daily Sentinel*, in 1903. In later years, it was renamed the *Grafton Sentinel*. As with many newspapers, it has evolved to meet the needs of the community. In 1975, it was purchased by the News Media Corporation, renamed to the *Mountain Statesman*, and switched from being a daily paper to printing three editions per week.

MOUNTAIN STATESMAN NEWSPAPER
PHOTO BY AUTHOR

GEORGE DUDDING

"...Robert Cockrell played a major part..."

In 1964, the *Grafton Sentinel* and one of its young newspaper reporters by the name of Robert Cockrell played a major part in the now famous Grafton Monster incident—the paper through its documentation of that event and the reporter through his keen sense of observation, research, reporting, and persistence in his search for the truth. Thanks to microfilm archives of the *Grafton Sentinel*, we were able to review two articles from that newspaper which helped to document that the whole incident did happen. Those archives are not found on file at the present newspaper facility, but instead, they are in the local library. The Mountain Statesman is headquartered at 914 West Main Street in Grafton. I was informed by the present editor that at the time of the monster incident, the *Grafton Sentinel* was located on Latrobe Street.

THE SIGHTING

It was around 11:00 PM on the fateful night of Tuesday, June 16, 1964 that a young reporter by the name of Robert Cockrell had just gotten off work at the *Grafton Sentinel* in Grafton, West Virginia. He had been working the evening shift and putting together a few last minute pieces of news before heading home. On that night, he didn't dream that he was about to enter the twilight zone and lock horns with his biggest news break of the year. If perhaps he could have been a clairvoyant, a sudden premonition might have made him pause just before pulling off the newspaper parking lot and choose a different route home. It could have saved him and a lot of others from the difficulties that later fell upon them. Instead, he navigated his car onto Beech Street, crossed the bridge over the Tygart River, and turned onto Riverside Drive, which runs parallel to the Tygart River.

"Something huge and white was standing along the side of the road..."

Cockrell accelerated to a speed of fifty miles per hour as he had driven the road many times, and he knew it like the back of his hand. Just as he came out of a long turn and entered a straight stretch of road, something suddenly caught his attention along the right side of the road near an old rock quarry. He let off the accelerator pedal to allow his car to slow down so he could take a closer look at what he saw. A stretch of ground lying between the roadway and the river had been recently mowed, which allowed the whole area along the riverbank to be distinctly visible in the high beams of his car headlights. Something huge and white was standing along the side of the road—not just some object, but a scary-looking, ugly monster. He applied his brakes sharply and craned his neck slightly toward the passenger side of the car to get a closer view. It was then that he realized that the thing was a living entity, white in color, with smooth, oily, slick skin. The texture of its skin reminded him of a seal. The best estimate of its height placed it between seven feet and nine feet tall. He observed the a hulk of a figure to be about four feet wide, but one thing that seemed to distinguish it from most monster creatures was the fact that it did not have a discernible head. As Cockrell drove his car right past the creature, it remained motionless in a stationary position. At no time during his momentary visual encounter did the creature try to escape, but Cockrell could tell that it was definitely alive.

Cockrell was so badly shaken by the late-night presence of such a huge, menacing creature standing along the side of the road that he stomped on the accelerator and sped the rest of the way to his home. Upon arriving at his house, he ran inside, slammed the door, and bolted it behind him. For the next half-hour, he was still nervous and shaking from the encounter, but he finally managed to get settled down and recover his thought processes. He began to think that in his role as a reporter that perhaps a more thorough investigation should be conducted. He thought carefully about the situation and wisely decided that he should not return to Riverside Drive alone. Instead, he called up a couple of friends, and they all drove back out to the location where he had seen the scary creature. A quick search of the encounter site along the riverbank revealed that the creature had made its getaway. No tracks were found, but the grass in one spot seemed to have been mashed down in such a manner to indicate that the entity might have rested its body there. Though, it was late at night, and they were working in low visibility. Cockrell and his associates continued to search the area up and down the road, along the riverbank, and in the edge of the woods throughout the next hour but still found nothing.

GEORGE DUDDING

They did notice something as they walked the riverbank, and that was a weird, low, whistling sound that came from somewhere nearby and seemed to follow them. It was later believed that the creature was watching them the whole time. On that night, the party was unable to determine the source of the noise, and they finally discontinued their search efforts and returned home with the intentions of going back again during the safety of daylight hours.

CITY OF GRAFTON HIGHWAY MARKER

The photographs taken by the author, shown on the following page, show the wide grassy area where the Grafton Monster was seen along the banks of the Tygart River on Riverside Drive.

THE GRAFTON MONSTER

RIVERSIDE DRIVE AND RIVERBANK
PHOTOS BY AUTHOR

THE FOLLOWING DAYS

On Wednesday morning, June 17, 1964, following the sighting, Cockrell arrived at the newspaper office and wondered what he was going to do with the story. He already knew that he would face opposition from his editor if he wrote up his story, and that is exactly what happened. He decided to take his story to the police, but they did not take it seriously as they often do not in reports of that nature. After speaking to his newspaper editor, it was suggested that he write up a short article, and it would be published in the next edition of the newspaper.

"They grabbed whatever they could find to protect themselves including pitchforks, mallets..."

By the end of the day, word had spread among the citizens of Grafton that a strange creature was stalking the banks of the Tygart River. The newspaper story was not due out until the following day, but Cockrell's two friends, Jim Mouser and Jerry Morse, had already leaked the story, which spread like wildfire. The story struck fear into the hearts of the local residents, and many of them foolishly went in search of the monster later that night. Dozens of teenagers and adults, without regard to personal safety, grabbed their flashlights and rushed to the banks of the Tygart River near the old rock quarry in what might be called a death wish. They were brave enough to participate in the hunt but also scared as evidenced by the weapons they carried. They grabbed whatever they could find to protect themselves including pitchforks, mallets, tire irons, hammers, garden hoes, crowbars, hatchets, pistols, knives, and baseball bats. If anyone knows about citizens of West Virginia, there is no doubt that some were toting some heavy-duty artillery that night. There were reports that several were carrying hunting rifles of various calibers, and at least one citizen was reported to have arrived with a 12-gauge shotgun. Some of the younger guys wanted to impress their girlfriends, so they brought them along. Others brought girls along in case they needed them for extra protection. With the mob mentality that existed among the crowd, it was actually a wonder that someone was not seriously hurt, which is one reason that law enforcement was concerned—the enormous amount of paperwork would have taken time out of their regular duties.

Cockrell appeared on the scene that night to gather as much information as possible. According to his collection of reports, over twenty witnesses claimed that they had seen the creature near the Tygart River or around the old stone quarry on that first night. Cockrell questioned as many of them as possible and recorded the details of their alleged encounters in his notebook. Afterwards, he composed the news article that his editor had requested earlier that day and presented it for publishing. A heavily edited version of his article, with many of the facts missing, appeared in the Thursday, June 18, 1964 edition of the *Grafton Sentinel*. The headlines read *Teen-Age Monster Hunting Parties Latest Activity on Grafton Scene*.

On Thursday night, following the first newspaper article, there was a repeat of the first night, only much more involved as motor traffic increased heavily along the river. It seemed that the whole community was now afflicted with a degree of mass hysteria. Cars lined the berm along Riverside Drive as enthusiastic monster hunters gathered to seek out the entity that had now become referred to as the "Headless Horror" or the "Beast of Grafton." Many of them loudly bragged as to how they planned to confront the monster head-on. In reality, they would have likely turned and run for their lives much like a hound dog with its tail tucked between its legs.

"Police had to give up on any real investigation of the incident and resort to working traffic control."

Word that a dangerous monster was roaming the woods around Grafton soon spread across the state. Law enforcement members of the West Virginia State Police, the Taylor County Sheriff's Department, and the Grafton Police Department were now forced to get involved and showed up to investigate. The officers fruitlessly searched the area for the monster, but they were careful to not drift too far from their squad cars. The worst fears of the law enforcement community became a reality as a rowdy group of monster hunters arrived on the scene carrying their weaponry. Hundreds of cars converged on Riverside Drive making it extremely congested by traffic. Police had to give up on any real investigation of the incident and resort to working traffic control. Luckily, there were no injuries or fatal accidents documented during the escapade that night.

Once again, Cockrell was on the scene with his pen and notepad. By the end of the second night, he had amassed a fairly substantial list of new sighting reports. None of them were quite as awesome as the encounter he had experienced only two nights before. Of course, there was no way of knowing if any of these new reports were of a questionable nature, but the witnesses seemed to be sure of what they had seen. With more information in hand, Cockrell returned to his office and wrote another story, which was to appear in the newspaper on the following day. Once again, the article was edited, and the story was slanted in a manner to discredit the witnesses. The Friday, June 19, 1964 *Grafton Sentinel* headlines read *"Monster" Result Of Spring Fever, Wild Imagination.*

EARLY THEORIES

Known as the "Headless Horror" in its earlier days, the name of the creature was eventually changed to the "Beast of Grafton" and later, the "Grafton Monster." Explanations for the strange sightings took on many forms such as the bizarre suggestion of a local teenager who thought it might have been a polar bear that had managed to get loose in the area without applying any thought as to how such an animal would have made its way there from the Arctic. The possibility that it had escaped from a zoo or circus was considered, but no zoo existed in the region, and no circus had frequented the area. Some believed that the monster might not be headless but was so large that, with its head held down low to its chest, it only appeared to be headless.

The Friday, June 19, 1964 edition of the *Grafton Sentinel* carried another short news article that claimed the monster was the "personification of the active imaginations of a number of teenagers" that was the "result of spring fever" and "wild imagination." The blame was placed on the fact that there were no recreational outlets for young people in the community. It also cited a similar monster sighting in Michigan that had recently made the news and could have possibly planted the whole monster idea in the minds of the witnesses. In the case of the two *Grafton Sentinel* newspaper articles that reported on the incident, both were censored by the editor for some reason and done so in a manner to cover up the true story of the monster as Cockrell had so carefully reported it. Cockrell had no idea what to do, but he soon developed another plan.

Local authorities who were in an urgency to quell the entire monster fiasco needed something else to discredit it. Another sighting came along just in time to meet their needs. A witness had seen someone pushing a cart, piled high with white boxes, along Riverside Drive late one night. The local newspaper placed a line in their story saying that the Grafton Monster had been the result of a misidentification of a cart load of boxes. This new revelation became an explanation for what had taken place, but Robert Cockrell new better. He later stated that he had seen some type of supernatural entity and not a stack of boxes.

A later story of similar nature claimed that a witness saw a local woman, believed to be a Betty Conrad, dragging a white refrigerator along the berm of Riverside Drive late one night. This story bears a resemblance to the cart of white boxes story. The exterior enameled surface of the refrigerator with its smoothly curved corners could have accounted for the white sealskin appearance of the monster. However, once again, this is not what Cockrell claimed to have witnessed. Moving a heavy refrigerator would have required a dolly or cart of some type. The cart load of boxes and the refrigerator story were not without merit, except for the fact that they had occurred several nights after the Cockrell sighting.

Then, there were the efforts to discredit Robert Cockrell by saying that he had made the whole incident up, possibly after hearing of the monster sighting in Michigan. One story was told that Cockrell saw a farmer's cow out roaming along the road at night and mistook it for something else. Such efforts to dispute eyewitness accounts are quite commonly used by skeptics in incidents of this type, and they are actually quite absurd.

"There is a tendency among law enforcement and military authorities to perpetrate cover-ups..."

There is a tendency among law enforcement and military authorities to perpetrate cover-ups in situations of this type to prevent the spread of mass panic. This seems to have taken place with the local law enforcement, the newspaper, and even city officials. Even with all the skeptics that crawled out of the woodwork, along with those who made every effort to debunk the story and discredit Cockrell's claims, the legend of the Grafton Monster still flourishes to this day.

GEORGE DUDDING

A DOLLY LOADED WITH WHITE BOXES

A NEWS REPORT CLAIMED THAT THE GRAFTON MONSTER WAS ACTUALLY A DOLLY LOADED WITH WHITE BOXES THAT WAS BEING PUSHED ALONG RIVERSIDE DRIVE.

THE GRAFTON MONSTER

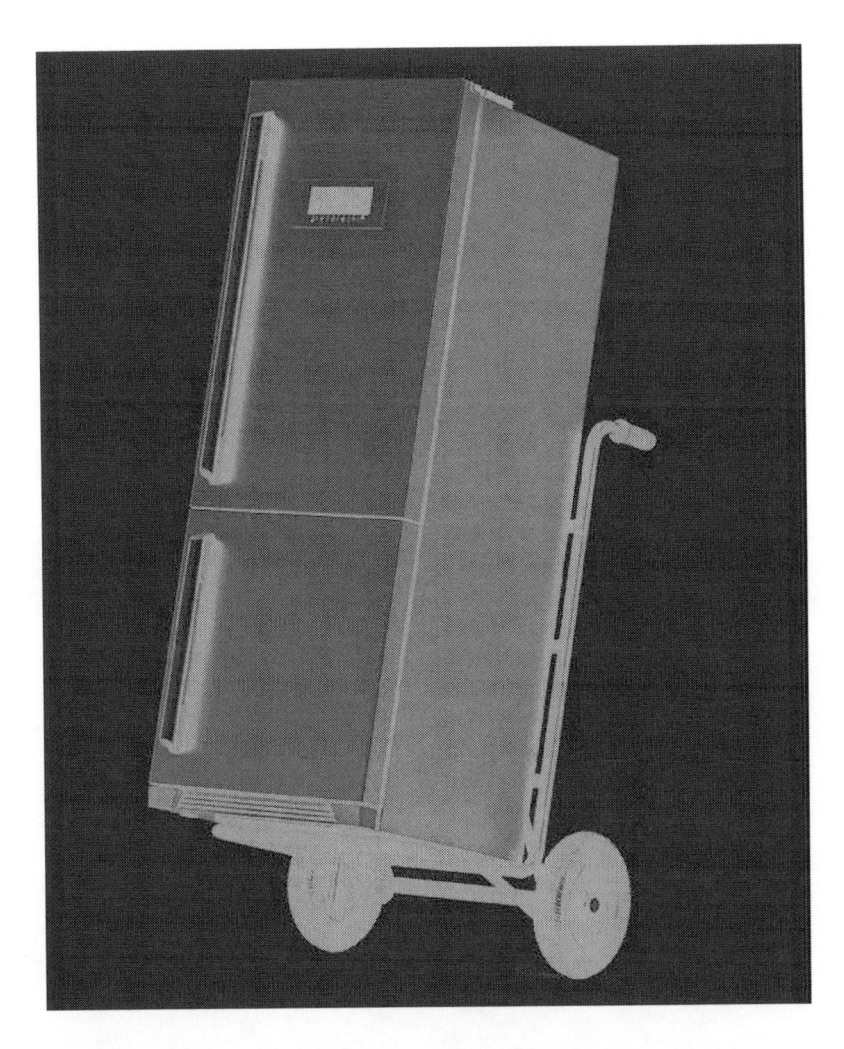

A DOLLY LOADED WITH A REFRIGERATOR

ANOTHER BIZARRE CLAIM STATED THAT A WOMAN WAS HAULING A REFRIGERATOR DOWN RIVERSIDE DRIVE AT 11 O'CLOCK AT NIGHT.

GEORGE DUDDING

NEWSPAPER CLIPPINGS

Teen-Age Monster Hunting Parties Latest Activity On Grafton Scene

Want to go "monster" hunting? If so just join the roving bands of teen-agers who are apparently convinced that a "monster" exists and is roving in the section of Riverside drive near the city stone quarry.

Wednesday night several bands of teen-agers armed with flashlights, mallets, crowbars, and the like, were reported searching the Riverside Drive area.

The description of the alleged Grafton "monster" sounds suspiciously like that of the recent reports of a "monster" in Michigan, except that Grafton's seems to be a bit bigger in every respect.

One teen-ager said that the youths on Wednesday night were searching for a creature "nine feet tall and about four feet wide." He said it is agreed that the creature is white, has no discernible head and emits a weird whistling sound.

So far as could be ascertained today, area law enforcement officials have taken no official notice of the reports of the Riverside drive "monster."

THE GRAFTON MONSTER

Several teen-agers, none of them identified by names, have reportedly "seen the monster" and given fairly tallying reports of its appearance.

The tale is even embellished with the theory that the creature was first sighted in the Morgantown area and arrived in the Riverside area via the Monongahela and Tygart rivers.

One youth suggested that it might be an escaped Polar bear but offered no suggestions as to where such an animal could have escaped.

"Monster" Result Of Spring Fever, Wild Imagination

Grafton's alleged "monster," reportedly the personification of the active imaginations of a number of teen-agers, couldn't have shown up in the Riverside drive area if it wanted to on Thursday night, too many teen-agers and adults were roamng that section of the city.

At approximately 10 p.m. it was reported that cars were almost bumper-to-bumper along the river drive and a large number of cars were pulled off the road to permit joining in the area's most popular sport in recent years "monster" hunting. Some 20 reports from persons allegedly seeing the

GEORGE DUDDING

"monster" have been quoted since Tuesday night when the "all white, creature without a discernible head," first was reported seen near the city rock quarry. Wednesday night about 30 teen-agers engaged in a "monster hunt," but by Thursday night the number of teen-agers had doubled and a number of adults joined in the action. A combination of spring fever, lack of area recreational facilities, and recent publicity given a Michigan town which claims to have a "monster" which followed people are believed to have laid the basis for the wildly imaginative story about a Grafton "monster."

A routine check by the sentinel showed that the "monster" story may have resulted from the fact that an individual pushing a handcart loaded high with boxes, walked along Riverside drive on Tuesday night. In the half-light of late evening, this person and the loaded handcart apparently took on a weird shape for persons having just read the story of the Michigan "monster."

"It's fairly certain that "monsters" don't go around pushing handcarts loaded with boxes.

THE PRECEDING ARTICLES ARE COURTESY OF THE FORMER GRAFTON SENTINEL NEWSPAPER

THE GRAFTON MONSTER

RIVERSIDE DRIVE WHERE MONSTER WAS SEEN
PHOTO BY JOHN DUDDING

SIMILAR SIGHTINGS

Even though the Grafton Monster was originally reported in Grafton in the mid-1960s, there have been indications that it was first seen during the 1950s and that other sightings also occurred elsewhere. During the intense period of Grafton Monster sightings that took place along the Tygart River in Taylor County, Robert Cockrell kept detailed notes on each of them. After the monster-craze died down, he doubled down on his investigation into the matter. The thought was considered that the monster sightings might have something to do with the rivers in the area.

The Tygart River flows northwestward from Grafton and joins with the West Fork River to become the Monongahela River before reaching Fairmont, West Virginia and then, flowing on to Morgantown, West Virginia. The Monongahela River is joined by the Cheat River at Point Marion, Pennsylvania and continues northward to where it flows into the Ohio River at Pittsburgh, Pennsylvania. Eventually, it all leads to the Mississippi River and down to the Gulf of Mexico. Cockrell felt that it was quite possible that the Grafton Monster had traveled there by way of this network of rivers.

Cockrell soon learned of other sightings of the slick-skinned monster that had taken place farther to the north. One had taken place downstream along the Monongahela River only 20 miles northward near Morgantown, West Virginia. He believed that it had gradually worked its way upstream and found its way south by following the rivers until he and others had seen it at Grafton.

One week prior to the Grafton sighting, a similar incident had made national news after being reported near Dowagiac, Michigan. On the night of June 9, 1964, a monster creature that was estimated to be ten feet tall and weighing 500 pounds was seen by several witnesses, including Mr. and Mrs. John Utrup, Patsy and Gail Clayton, Gordon Brown, and Joyce Smith, at the Utrup farm south of Dewey Lake.

Dewey Lake is a 174-acre lake that is one of a group of ten lakes in the unincorporated community of Sister Lakes in Cass County, Michigan. As a result, the monster became known as the "Dewey Lake Monster." Around 30 additional sightings later occurred and included one on June 11, 1964 when three girls encountered it along a road during daylight hours. It was believed that the monster inhabited a fifteen-mile area of swampy land that lies mostly along Dewey Lake Street between Sister Lakes and Decatur, Michigan. Bizarre stories were even told that it lived beneath the surface of the water in Dewey Lake and was amphibious. Eventually, it was determined to be a Bigfoot-like creature that became known as the "Michigan Bigfoot" or the "Sister Lakes Sasquatch." In a strange coincidence, an article about the Dewey Lake monster was featured in the *Grafton Sentinel* only one week prior to Cockrell's encounter with the Grafton creature.

"His father asked him to go to the truck and retrieve a double-barrel shotgun..."

Around that same time, another witness that lived 800 miles away near St. Joseph, Missouri, recalled seeing a monster of the same description along the Missouri River. The Missouri River also happens to be a tributary to the Mississippi River and, therefore, is in the network of rivers that were mentioned earlier. The witness claimed that he had seen the strange entity several times and subsequently told the story of two separate encounters that he had incurred. In one case, he and his father were cutting firewood in the woods when a sudden outburst of barking from their dogs alerted them that something was approaching. After shutting off their chainsaws, they could hear the sounds of heavy footsteps in the nearby woods. His father asked him to go to the truck and retrieve a double-barrel shotgun loaded with double-ought buckshot. He returned with the gun just as some type of huge creature stepped out of the trees about 150 feet from them. It paused for a bit, turned around, and walked back into the woods. Both men were severely shaken by what they had seen. The witness did not know it at the moment, but he would soon have a second encounter.

It was a couple of months later that the witness had his second encounter while fishing along the bank of a waterway near the Missouri River. It was early in the morning when the witness saw the monster not far away on the opposite bank from where he was fishing. The monster went motionless and did not move. The witness promptly abandoned his fishing equipment, ran to his truck, and prepared to leave the area. As the witness turned to look back toward the creature, he observed it running away. The weird part of the encounter came as the witness heard a strange "whooshing sound" followed by a bright ball of light rising above the trees and lifting off into the sky. The witness jumped into his truck and drove away without hesitation. He was so scared that he waited for two days before returning to get his fishing equipment. The witness made an assessment of both encounters and felt that the entity wasn't afraid of human presence because it didn't immediately break and run, yet it didn't offer to approach and attack at any time. The witness felt that it was best to not stay around and find out if it were dangerous. The report made by the witness also revealed another piece of strange information—the possibility that a UFO had rendezvoused with the creature, picked it up, and lifted off into the sky leaving behind a trail of light and a cosmic sound.

The monster that was sighted in Missouri is now believed to be the same creature known as "Momo." Lyle Blackburn recently released a new book, *Momo: The Strange Case of the Missouri Monster*, that provides more details on the creature.

"In the early 1960s, West Virginia was visited by a barrage of other strange bipedal creatures."

THE GRAFTON MONSTER

An article written by Thomas Stafford in the September 21, 1952 edition of the *Raleigh Register* reported on another monster that Robert Cockrell felt matched the description of the Grafton Monster. A woman named Mrs. Hutchinson had witnessed a sighting near the unincorporated community of Skelton about two miles north of Beckley, West Virginia in Raleigh County. She saw the entity in the sky and described it as being a large, shiny, white creature resembling a washtub. The witness described the motion of the object as occasionally moving up and down and then, swinging back and forth. At the time, the sighting was equated with the Flatwoods Monster incident of Braxton County that had occurred 70 miles away and about a week earlier, but it did not come close to meeting the description of that particular entity. Interestingly, a washing machine might have sounded more appropriate than a washtub, because it would have more closely resembled a refrigerator like the one allegedly seen along Riverside Drive. The Skelton sighting actually sounded more like a UFO than a monster creature.

AUTHOR'S NOTE: The Flatwoods Monster was a strange entity, witnessed by six boys and one woman, that emerged from a flying saucer or UFO after landing on a hilltop at Flatwoods, West Virginia on the night of September 12, 1952. That incident is covered in another of my books, The Flatwoods Monster.

    In the early 1960s, West Virginia was visited by a barrage of other strange bipedal creatures. Something called the Apple Devils made a regular appearance in Pocahontas County near Marlinton. These strange entities were picking the apples off trees in orchards and leaving behind damaged fruit trees, fences, and other farm appurtenances. It was later believed that they were a Bigfoot-Sasquatch kind of creature.

    In the summer of 1960, W. C. Priestly and some friends were in the Marlinton, West Virginia area on a fishing expedition. Priestly encountered a strange Bigfoot-type creature along the road, and his car simultaneously stalled. The creature vanished into the woods, and his car was able to be restarted. Only a few minutes later, farther along the road, he encountered the same entity again, and a repeat performance ensued as his car engine malfunctioned once again until the creature vanished into the woods for its final time.

    Other bizarre sightings of bipedal Bigfoot-type monsters took place during the summer of

THE GRAFTON MONSTER

1960 in the Monongahela Forest at the West Virginia towns of Parsons and Davis. These creatures stood around eight feet tall and had shaggy fur.

Another sighting of a hairy, bipedal monster occurred in December of 1960 near Hickory Flats, West Virginia on the border between Braxton and Webster Counties. In that case, a bread truck driver by the name of Charles Stover almost collided with the monster after rounding a sharp turn on a desolate secondary road.

Several of the above encounters are further detailed in my book, *Bigfoot West Virginia*. These and other appearances of strange humanoid creatures around West Virginia during the same time frame have elicited proposals that the Grafton Monster might actually be a Bigfoot-Sasquatch type of creature, or possibly be related to them.

Unfortunately, news was often censored at the *Grafton Sentinel*, and Robert Cockrell never converted his collection of Grafton Monster sighting reports and notes into an article so they could be published. This didn't stop the legend of the Grafton Monster, over the next half-century, from becoming embedded in the colorful and sometimes scary Appalachian folklore and stories of West Virginia.

GRAY BARKER

Gray Roscoe Barker (1925–1984) grew up near the community of Riffle, West Virginia in Braxton County not far from Flatwoods. He graduated from Glenville State College in 1947 and taught English for a short time. He entered the movie theater business at Clarksburg, West Virginia and operated his own theater. Eventually, he formed and ran a business of booking films for movie and drive-in theaters. His fame is credited to his work of investigating and writing about UFOs. He created and published his own UFO magazine, the *Saucerian*, which later became *The Saucerian Bulletin*. He also wrote articles for several magazines including *FATE*, *Space Review*, and *Flying Saucers*. He was the author of the book *They Knew Too Much About Flying Saucers* along with another book *Silver Bridge* that attempted to establish a link between the 1967 bridge disaster and the 1966 appearance of "Mothman" at Point Pleasant, West Virginia. He was an early pioneer in research of the mysterious beings known as the "Men in Black" and wrote a final book titled *MIB: The Secret Terror Among Us*. Barker was also known for his 1952 investigation of the Flatwoods Monster UFO incident near his hometown in Braxton County.

"He was an early pioneer in research of the mysterious beings known as the "Men in Black"…"

After his encounter with the Grafton Monster, Robert Cockrell's next step in furthering his investigations was to get in contact with Gray Barker. Barker was conveniently located only twenty miles away in Clarksburg and promptly made a special trip to Grafton to meet up, interview, and visit the site along Riverside Drive where the monster had been seen.

Barker proposed that perhaps the monster seen by Cockrell and twenty other witnesses, including several teenagers, was something that had arrived here from another planet by way of a flying saucer. He thought that the strange creature might have been a test entity that had been dropped off in advance of other visitors from space to test the livability of the Earth's surface and atmosphere before others could safely emerge from their craft and set foot on Earth. Barker suggested that the low whistling sounds heard by witnesses along the river were emitted by a flying saucer hovering nearby while waiting to retrieve the entity. This is consistent with early science fiction films where cosmic sound effects were employed when flying saucers were in flight. Several UFO sightings had been reported by residents of Grafton around the time of the monster sightings.

Barker apparently wrote up the story with the intentions of placing it in a UFO magazine, but for some strange reason, it was never published. Some have theorized that he might have not published the story out of concern that it was a hoax, but this would most likely have not mattered because Barker was known on occasion to be a hoaxer himself. The rough draft of the article, along with newspaper clippings, notes, and correspondence related to the case, were later discovered in Barker's collection of documents, publications, and memorabilia located in a room, appropriately named the Gray Barker Room, at the Clarksburg-Harrison Public Library in Clarksburg, West Virginia.

AN INTERPLANETARY ALIEN

During the flying saucer craze of the late 1940s up through the early 1960s, some believed that an alien might travel here from a nearby planet within our solar system, or even a planet belonging to a different solar system located someplace else in our galaxy. Just how could an alien ship travel great distances to get here from such a planet?

One thought that is based upon Einstein's *special theory of relativity* and an application of the Lorentz transformations is that an alien spaceship in motion exhibits time dilation when seen by an observer from a stationary frame of reference. Also, that same spaceship would exhibit length contraction when seen by the same observer from a stationary frame of reference. A third effect that the spaceship would undergo would be a relativistic mass increase. When applied to a moving ship, time dilation, length contraction, and mass increase are practically unnoticeable at slower speeds but increase dramatically as the moving ship approaches the speed of light. By length contraction, we mean the ship would become shorter in length, and by time dilation, we mean that time would pass slower on board the ship. The relativistic mass increase means that as the speed of the ship increases, kinetic energy would be converted to mass, resulting in an increase of the mass of the spacecraft.

A craft traveling from Mars at the speed of light, 186,000 miles per second, could reach Earth in a matter of minutes. Spacecrafts, such as those launched by NASA, traveling at 36,000 miles per hour, would require about 300 days to make such a trip. We now realize that any alien on the level of our monster is not likely to be from a nearby planet because the environment on other planets in our solar system is too hostile. However, it is likely that such an alien could exist on planets in other solar systems. For example, such a solar system could be located at Alpha Centauri, the nearest star in our galaxy. Logically, it would seem that since Alpha Centauri is located 4.3 light-years from Earth, an alien ship traveling at the speed of light would require 4.3 years to reach Earth. That is a long time, but it is even much longer if the star was one million light-years away requiring one million years to make the trip—so it would seem.

"…there is a way such a craft piloted by aliens could make the trip across interstellar space in a shorter time."

Perhaps, there is a way such a craft piloted by aliens could make the trip across interstellar space in a shorter time. Imagine that you are a passenger on a train traveling toward the next town. You know that the train tracks and the

THE GRAFTON MONSTER

ground upon which they rest are stationary, and the train is moving—at least that is what an observer on the ground sees. You may have ridden on a train or even watched it in the movies. If you are looking out the passenger train window, it appears that telephone poles adjacent to the tracks are flying past your window toward the rear of the train. It would appear to you that the train is stationary and the telephone poles, the land next to the tracks, and even the tracks are moving past the train, and also, the next town is moving toward the train. If you consider the train stationary and the tracks to be moving, then the tracks will appear to undergo length contraction. The distance from the train to the next town will be shortened. A clock on the church tower in that town will also seem to run slower because of time dilation. You, the passenger on the train, have placed yourself and the train in a stationary frame of reference. You are viewing the train tracks as being in the moving frame of reference.

"...the distance of 4.3 light-years shrinks to a distance that can be traversed in only a few hours, minutes, or even seconds!"

Now, return to the alien craft traveling from Alpha Centauri toward Earth. If the craft could approach light speed, then it might seem that it would take about 4.3 years to make the trip. But there is another factor in which the aliens on the craft can be placed in the stationary frame of reference and interstellar space is racing past them at near the speed of light. The distance between Alpha Centauri and Earth undergoes length contraction, and the distance of 4.3 light-years shrinks to a distance that can be traversed in only a few hours, minutes, or even seconds!

The above theory does have its limitations. According to Einstein's special theory of relativity, the mass of the ship would increase infinitely as it approaches light speed, and the additional mass would come from the conversion of kinetic energy to mass—a large amount of energy would be required to approach the necessary speed to accomplish such a space flight.

The following elementary formulas are included for the mathematically adept. They describe the concept of special relativity discussed above where v = the speed of the spaceship, c = the speed of light, t = stationary time, l = stationary length, m = stationary mass, t' = dilated time, l' = contracted length, and m' = mass increase.

Time dilation	$t' = t\sqrt{1 - \dfrac{v^2}{c^2}}$
Length contraction	$l' = l\sqrt{1 - \dfrac{v^2}{c^2}}$
Mass increase	$m' = \dfrac{m}{\sqrt{1 - \dfrac{v^2}{c^2}}}$

SPECIAL THEORY OF RELATIVITY FORMULAS

If the difficulties mentioned above cannot be ironed out, perhaps there is another way in which the travel time between interstellar planets might be shortened significantly. What if there was a shortcut between different locations in the universe? Such shortcuts might exist in the form of an anomaly called a "wormhole." Our twisted, warped universe of possibly at least eleven dimensions, supported by a theory covered in the next section, is predicted to contain such passageways linking different points in space-time. Those pathways could serve as a shortcut between our solar system and another. They are also predicted by Einstein's *general theory of relativity*.

GEORGE DUDDING

AN INTERDIMENSIONAL ALIEN

Some have theorized that the Grafton Monster may have been some type of intelligent, *interdimensional* being from a different universe or reality other than our own. Such beings are common in fantasy, science fiction, and the supernatural. An attempt to explain how this might work is presented in the following paragraphs by using some mathematical concepts of which you are probably familiar, accompanied by some theoretical physics.

Basically, our universe can be explained through the use of dimensions which tell us where we are located relative to everything else. Referring to what we have learned in basic algebra, we know that a point can be located along a straight line (number line) by a single coordinate (x). This location is one-dimensional. By adding a second number line we can describe the location of that point more precisely on a flat surface (plane) with two coordinates (x,y). This location is two-dimensional. If we add a third number line, we can further locate a point even more precisely in space using three coordinates (x,y,z). This is three-dimensional. By adding time to the scheme, we can locate a point not only in space but also in time using four coordinates

(x,y,z,t). This is four-dimensional. You may have watched some of the older science fiction movies in which time travel was referred to as "traveling in the fourth dimension."

"These additional dimensions could also give us other universes or multiverses..."

With the recent advent of a new theory by physicists called *Super String Theory*, we can add six more dimensions for a total of ten. Still yet, another theory called *M-theory* gives us an additional dimension for a total of eleven. Some of these dimensions are visualized as straight lines, while some might be thought of as being twisted around others. It is believed that these additional dimensions could unite the theories of electromagnetism and gravity. These additional dimensions could also give us other universes or multiverses, sometimes referred to as "parallel universes." This concept could allow other worlds to co-exist undetected right here with our universe because they are running along different "time lines."

The possibility is opened up for cryptids, UFOs, and other things to slip between these different universes by way of "wormholes" or similar anomalies in the "space-time fabric." This could explain the occasional sudden appearance and disappearance of certain mysterious objects and creatures such as Bigfoot, Mothman, UFOs, and the elusive Grafton Monster. Also, the passing of creatures between dimensions could result in the bending of the "space-time fabric" thereby producing electromagnetic distortions. Since light is an electromagnetic phenomena, distortion of those light rays could result in the blurry and distorted photographs we see with Bigfoot and other such creatures or entities.

In the case of the Grafton Monster, as the need arose, it may have been able to momentarily slip in and out of our universe in such a way as to become invisible to Cockrell, his friends, and later the crowd of monster hunters that came out on the following night at the riverbank. The low whistling sounds that were heard by witnesses along the river are believed by interdimensional theorists to have been the sound of the monster switching between universes.

Admittedly, the scenarios set forth in this and the previous section may sound a little farfetched, but since my college degrees are centered on physics and mathematics, I am putting the ideas out there.

THE MEN IN BLACK

During my research into the Grafton Monster incident, it appeared to me that a cover-up had taken place at different stages of the event, and there are others who feel the same. After digging through old files that were used in the writing of my earlier books, I was able to find information that enabled me to develop a possible theory. It revolves around strange entities that manage to show up at the most inconvenient times and try to squelch any release of information about UFOs and related strange occurrences.

An early incident involving such entities was first reported by Harold Dahl in June of 1947 after a dangerous encounter with several UFOs while operating a boat in the Puget Sound at Maury Island in the State of Washington, USA. On the very next day, Dahl was confronted at his home by a strange man, dressed in black, who warned him to not discuss the matter with anyone. Dahl ignored the strange warning and reported the UFO incident to the authorities.

In 1953, Albert Bender, founder of the *International Flying Saucer Bureau* and publisher of *Space Review* magazine, was about to publish an article on UFO cover-ups in an October issue. He was visited by three men, dressed in black, who warned him to not publish any more information about flying saucers. Bender took the warning seriously, disbanded the International Flying Saucer Bureau and did not publish the article. Gray Barker had been publishing his work in Space Review and questioned Bender about what had happened. In 1956, Barker's investigation into the matter resulted in the publishing of a book, *They Knew Too Much about Flying Saucers*, that was about these strange agents dressed in black. Barker became the first to coin the phrase "men in black" when describing these weirdos. In 1963, Bender made a comeback and wrote a book, *Flying Saucers and the Three Men*, which was about these strange entities.

The men in black continued to be a nuisance by appearing in Point Pleasant, West Virginia around the time of the Mothman sightings that took place there in 1966. Mary Hyre, a correspondent newspaper reporter for the *Athens Messenger*, had been covering a rash of UFO sightings that were occurring in the area. She was visited by peculiar-acting men, dressed in black, who strongly discouraged her from investigating and writing about flying saucers. Soon, others in the community experienced similar visits from the dark strangers that have become known as the *Men in Black*.

THE GRAFTON MONSTER

In the case of the Grafton Monster, we have the failure of Robert Cockrell's editor to publish the full story as he reported it. Cockrell later provided his full story to Gray Barker with the understanding that it would be published in Space Review magazine, but it still never happened. As years passed, the full story never made it into the news. It has even been said that Robert Cockrell withdrew and repudiated his own story of the event. This seems like a good time to invoke my theory. Could the notorious Men in Black have visited several key players in this incident and persuaded them to keep quiet?

FALLOUT 76

Ted Fauster, billed on Amazon as an award winning author of contemporary fantasy fiction, published a thirteen-page digital book on August 13, 2014. The work, titled *Cullen MacGregor's Last Hunt*, is packed with the adventures of a survivalist struggling to survive in West Virginia after a nuclear attack destroys everything in the surrounding states. Due to its mountainous terrain, much of West Virginia was spared from the apocalyptic damage. Fauster conjures up a few of the more well-known West Virginia folkloric monsters throughout the book. It is believed that the theme of his book led to the development of a suddenly-popular game called *Fallout 76*.

"Players of the game are already confronting legendary West Virginia creatures such as..."

In 2018, Bethesda Game Studios, creators of the games Skyrim and Fallout 4, introduced a new game, *Fallout 76*. The object of the game is to survive in a wasteland that is left over after the United States has undergone nuclear annihilation. The game takes place in West Virginia, and players must confront situations based upon geographic regions, folklore, and their associated monsters, but they better watch out. Some of the monsters seem to be going out of their generally known jurisdiction in an all out effort to annihilate the redneck hillbillies—I mean the perfectly normal citizens—of Appalachia. Players of the game are already confronting legendary West Virginia creatures such as Mothman, Flatwoods Monster, Snallygaster, Mole Man, Mega Sloth, Wendigo, and last but not least, this book's namesake—the Grafton Monster.

MOUNTAIN MONSTERS

In 2013, a new television series, *Mountain Monsters*, premiered on Destination America, a cable TV channel owned by Discovery, Inc. On each show, the Appalachian Investigators of Mysterious Sightings (AIMS) team, consisting of six West Virginia mountain men, travels throughout Appalachia in their attempt to prove the existence of unidentified creatures whose existence is denied by the scientific community. These creatures, known as cryptids, are the subject of study by cryptozoologists. Each episode of the program features another new cryptid. Among the list of creatures that have been featured on the show are Bigfoot, Lizard Man, Mothman, Werewolf, Hellhound, and the one in this book—the Grafton Monster.

In *Mountain Monsters* Season 2, Episode 2 (2014), the AIMS team journeyed to the area around Grafton in Taylor County to investigate the "huge bipedal predator" known as the "Headless Horror" or Grafton Monster. As they travelled to the location, the ultimate of hillbilly-type characters, Trapper, Jeff, Huckleberry, and Buck, discussed the creature, its history, and where it had been recently seen. Upon their arrival in Taylor County, the AIMS team met up with their first eyewitness, a cattle farmer named Wolfie, who was not only able to direct them to a specific location where he had recently seen the Grafton Monster but also showed them an actual video that he had taken of the monster chasing several of his best Black Angus cattle.

The AIMS team then went on a preliminary nighttime hunt to try and get a handle on what is going on in the woods around Grafton. They were in luck when they were able to spot the creature on a thermal imaging camera and track him to where he had climbed to the top of someone's deer stand and made a bloody meal out of a calf. It must have been a really grizzly scene for those who were unfortunate enough to have been there with these TV actors.

"While on the scene, they had the wits scared out of them by a deep growl..."

The following day, the team met up with Dale, a deer hunter that was able to show them a trail camera picture of the monster, a plaster cast that he had taken of its footprint, and the area where it was last seen. Next, they went to visit one more witness, Doc, and accompanied him to where he had seen the monster crossing a power line right-of-way. While on the scene, they had the wits scared out of them by a deep growl heard coming from the nearby woods.

A plan to hunt and capture the monster was concocted by the brains of the group, while expert trap builders, Willie and Wild Bill, cut down trees to harvest the logs necessary to construct the biggest box trap known to man—big enough to hold a nine-foot-tall, 1,500-pound beast.

With the giant wood trap completed and bait placed inside, the AIMS team came together, complete with an arsenal of firearms, for a final nighttime hunt in the woods. The team soon picked up the monster's trail in the thick underbrush and began driving him through the woods until they found evidence that he had just caught a deer and dragged it to the top of an oil tank, ate most of it, and left the mutilated remains of its carcass for them to find. It was then that the AIMS team realized that they might no longer be the hunters, but might have become the hunted.

In the final, scary moments of the hunt, the AIMS team tracked the creature back to their trap, just as they had intended, but the creature had been smarter than they had expected. The Grafton Monster had climbed to the top of their trap, and rather than enter through the trap door, it had pulled the bait out through the top of the trap and consumed it. Then, the monster was heard growling in the distance. The AIMS team had some choice words about the situation as they came to full realization that the Grafton Monster had outwitted them and made its getaway. It wasn't the first time this had happened to the team, and it wouldn't be the last.

AUTHOR'S NOTE: Much of the information, descriptions, and habits of the Grafton Monster as seen on the Mountain Monsters TV program should not be taken seriously and definitely not used as evidence of the creature's existence. Some believe that everything depicted on the program is the gospel, but others suspect that much of the program is staged and sensationalized purely for the purpose of entertaining its audience.

It is disturbing that other investigators and researchers have gone to both the Fallout 76 game and the Mountain Monsters reality TV show to accumulate facts and information about the real Grafton Monster.

THE GRAFTON MONSTER

A LOCAL COFFEE SHOP

A local coffee shop called *Expresso Yourself* is located at 34 West Main Street in Grafton. It seems to be a place where local Grafton Monster aficionados like to hang out, get something to eat or drink and talk about the creature. If you are there at the right time on the right day, you may possibly meet some of them.

COFFEE SHOP WE VISITED IN GRAFTON
PHOTO BY AUTHOR

Other cryptid researchers and paranormal investigators who make the pilgrimage to Grafton are known to stop off at this friendly place to gather and talk. Book authors, graphic artists, photographers, film makers, and others often stop there when making their rounds checking out the monster-infested communities of West Virginia.

While I had a good conversation with a graphic artist during my visit at the coffee shop, I was able to obtain more useful information by talking to elderly citizens, around lunchtime, on the parking lot of the Taylor County Senior Citizens Center located south of Grafton on U.S. Route 119. We must remember that the teenagers and adults present on Riverside Drive the night after the encounter would now be age seventy or older. One of the things they are good at is taking out the time to reminisce the good old days when they were still teenagers growing up in Grafton.

GRAFTON MONSTER BILLBOARD

With the recent attention give to the Grafton Monster by the Destination America TV show, *Mountain Monsters,* and the Bethesda game, *Fallout 76,* several community-minded citizens decided that Grafton needed to take advantage of the tourism opportunity by erecting a billboard along Riverview Drive to direct attention to the very location where newspaper reporter Robert Cockrell had sighted the monster over a half-century earlier.

A group of locals worked together on the project of funding, designing, and creating a suitable billboard. Together, they went out to the site along Riverview Drive and erected the billboard and its supporting structure. After the billboard sign was erected, there was a surge in tourism as visitors came from afar to have their pictures taken alongside the sign. It didn't take long for at least one nefarious individual to find another use for the magnificent sign.

"…the Grafton Monster banner was removed from its support frame and carried away."

Everything went well until Sunday, November 25, 2018, between midnight and 2:30 AM, when the Grafton Monster banner was removed from its support frame and carried away. Some locals, most likely out late at night looking for the monster, were driving along Riverside Drive when they noticed that the sign was missing from its usual perch. They hauled out their smartphones and immediately notified

GEORGE DUDDING

the billboard sponsors and the local authorities of their discovery. A local TV station announced that local Grafton Monster fans were downright outraged that someone had stolen the sign.

MISSING BILLBOARD
PHOTO BY JOHN DUDDING

Law enforcement sprung into action as they searched for any clues that might lead to the apprehension of the criminals and possible recovery of the billboard banner. Those who were primarily involved in placing the billboard just hoped to have the sign returned unharmed. A local political figure indicated that it was highly unlikely that local kids would commit such an act, while others wondered why such possibilities

THE GRAFTON MONSTER

should be ruled out. Some surmised that perhaps the Grafton Monster himself had returned to remove the sign in an effort to keep the location of its territory a secret from curious spectators. The Sheriff of Taylor County, Terry A. Austin, along with his deputies, the Grafton City Police, and the West Virginia State Police, soon picked up a lead on who had perpetrated the crime. It was learned that a West Virginia University student had removed the billboard banner and taken it to Morgantown to be displayed on the wall in his dormitory room.

Law enforcement made arrangements to have the banner returned, but it had suffered some damage because it had been folded. They figured that it had been folded to fit in inside the perpetrator's car. According to a news source, authorities were considering at least sentencing the student to a period of community service for his dastardly deed. While investigating, the author was able to learn a few details on who committed the act, but that part has no application in this book. Meanwhile, donations were collected locally and nationwide for replacement of the banner and also for some type of lighting system so it could be more easily viewed at night. The possibility of video surveillance was also given consideration. As of

April 2019, when this author visited Riverside Drive, it was observed that the billboard banner was either not replaced, or it had been stolen again. An inquiry around town revealed that the new banner had not yet been replaced as there was a concern that someone would take it again.

CONCLUSION

When concluding books of this nature, I like to give one final warning. If you are venturing out into any wilderness area for the purpose of conducting your own private investigation into any strange cryptid such as the Grafton Monster, do not trespass on private property, and be sure to follow all applicable laws. Do not venture out alone. You can easily become lost, fall in the water, fall off a cliff, fall into a sinkhole, or experience medical problems.

"...never fall into the misguided belief that any of these weird monsters want to be your friend."

If you would happen to encounter any strange creature along the road, in the woods, or anywhere else, do not take any chances. You never know what an entity like that is capable of doing, especially if it feels that its territory is being threatened. Most important of all—never fall into the misguided belief that any of these weird monsters want to be your friend. You could be in for a surprise that could lead to your demise.

THE END

GEORGE DUDDING

PRE-RELEASE REVIEWS

I personally appreciate the author's efforts to provide a little history about the community.
–Local historian

More input into this book should have been given to the local government officials.
–Local politician

I would much rather read a good comic book. At least it would probably have better content.
–Unacknowledged

The monster was probably a giant porcupine that lost all of its quills through the process of evolution.
–John Daniels

I always enjoy reading Dudding's books, because he incorporates local history into his work. After working with him, I realize how much effort he puts into adding a little historical background. I have read all 52 of his books, and I always look forward to the next.
–Liz LaMac

This author has penned another book that I find enjoyable to read.
–Loyal fan

THE GRAFTON MONSTER

1890s HOME IN GRAFTON
LIBRARY OF CONGRESS

OTHER BOOKS BY THIS AUTHOR

Strange Encounters: UFOs, Aliens and Mothman
The Tale of the Mason County Mothman
If I Taught It
The Flatwoods Monster
What Happened at Roswell?
They Haunt the Winfield Cemetery
The Kecksburg UFO Incident
The Kelly-Hopkinsville UFO and Alien Shootout
The Rendlesham Forest UFO
The Cape Girardeau 1941 UFO Incident
The Aurora 1897 UFO-Alien Encounter
The Socorro UFO Close Encounter
Bigfoot: The West Virginia Foothold
The Shag Harbour UFO Puzzle
The Berwyn Mountain UFO
The Thomas Mantell UFO Encounter
Sis Linn: The Ghost of Glenville State College
The Arnoldsburg Molasses Monster (not in print)
The Spencer Black Walnut Monster (not in print)
Inside Haunted Spencer State Hospital
Bigfoot 2: The West Virginia Stomping Grounds
The Aztec Flying Saucer Affair
The Laredo UFO Crash
Bigfoot 3: The West Virginia Toehold
The Silver Bridge Tragedy
The Falcon Lake UFO Encounter
Sheepsquatch
Bigfoot 4: The West Virginia Footprint
Kentucky's Lake Herrington Monster

THE GRAFTON MONSTER

The Maury Island UFO Encounter
Return to Haunted Spencer State Hospital
Dogman: Michigan-Wisconsin-West Virginia
The Cash Landrum UFO Encounter
The Levelland UFO Case
Goatman
Ohio's Frogmen and Melon Heads
Beyond Haunted Spencer State Hospital
Bigfoot 5: The West Virginia Yeti
Devil Monkey
Crybaby Bridge
Spring-heeled Jack
Cemetery Ghost Hunting: An Investigative Approach
The Oceana Monster
Cemetery Ghost Hunting 2: More Investigations
History of Spencer State Hospital
The Jersey Devil
Haunted White House
Graveyard Ghost Hunting: The Search Continues
Bigfoot West Virginia
Haunted Highways USA
Abraham Lincoln: The Ghost Years
The Grafton Monster
Haunted Savannah
UFO Traffic Stop
The Snarly Yow
Mothman Territory: History and High Strangeness
Skunk Ape: Florida's Bigfoot
Krazy House: America's Haunted Asylums
Dover Demon and Pukwudgies

Made in the USA
Middletown, DE
25 September 2022